GHOST CAMERA

GHOST CAMERA

POEMS

DAVID SEMANKI

TURNING POINT
CINCINNATI, OHIO

Published by Turning Point
P.O. Box 541106
Cincinnati, OH 45254-1106

FIRST EDITION

ISBN: 9781625494573

Poetry Editor: Kevin Walzer
Business Editor: Lori Jareo
Visit us on the Web at www.turningpointbooks.com.

Interior Design: Gretchen Achilles

For Eddie

CONTENTS

GHOST CAMERA

i see both worlds:

prescription(s)
                              for anxiety.

—where is
                this soul's   house?

in metaphors   on nitrate film stock.

o fugitive.
                        ghost.

KINDRED

DOMESTIC GOTHIC

it's snowing. so
brother goes out to shovel.

the winter routine.

too young to help.
i am sent to play
in snowsuit and boots.

a plow moves down the street,
sounds of gravel being scraped,

then tinny silence,
more snow mounds, endless—

from that pliable white material
i carve walls, ceiling, and floor.
a new home.

inside the fragile fort,
i am invisible; i disappear:

no body or barrier,
no season or time,
no other.

can't be found, can't
be hurt.

crawling back out, nothing was milder.
the world waited for me.

brother chips at ice on the front steps.
a path has been cleared from house to car.
cold built into the design.

(on the cement sidewalk,
a young father balances his toddler son
on his shoulders
as he walks home.

family is joy and burden, both
bearing equal weight.

true dusk. dinnertime.

the two enter the house's wide wooden front door
as the porch light flips on.

the light, a symbol of caretaking. if you dream.

dream that
a child could be safe.)

school vacation. days lengthen.

saturday afternoon sunlight
floods the backyard and garden.

patio blocks—muted pinks, saturated yellows.

done with chores, i read *jane eyre*
in order to watch the movie.

father sits in pine shade
drinking a glass of ice tea, then smokes his pipe.

the family poodle mix sleeps on fresh cut lawn.

contentment
as stasis, not action.

the same scene—

here it would be forgivable
to see this static world

as unified, a mirage
in the mind's eye
that all is not fractured.

identical to other houses along the narrow avenue,
an air conditioner hums
in an inconspicuous back window.

the same scene
ceasing, repeating, ceasing. circular like childhood games,
like musical chairs
i once played.

a game of refusal. i learned one's only defense,
play with vengeance.

BIOPIC, DADDY

teutonic wolves march through a ukrainian border town.
my father is slapped across his seven-year-old face
by a nazi soldier for failing to salute.
the black-capped officer in charge does not touch anyone;
he wants to keep his claws clean.

from the heights of a top bunk, i hear the television score of *the world at war*.
the sober narrating of laurence olivier

becomes my father's voice. i fall asleep, straining
to listen.

GHOST IN THE GRAVEYARD

a town of ruin and roses—

forgotten train tracks
segmented the large graveyard. the oldest tombstones
bordered road.

worn letters, lives rubbed out
with butcher paper and charcoal or colored wax.

youth and curiosity brought
the neighborhood boys together.

they take turns being "it,"
being "ghost,"
being the one who doesn't have to hide.

these boys grow literal in the graveyard.

ghost's duty is to hunt down players
and kiss them
before they reach the safety of home base.

this act of kissing another neighborhood boy
is acknowledged
as punishment, as deep embarrassment.

only occasionally game time is interrupted
by an appearance of the groundskeeper's green truck.

when i become ghost, i want to remain ghost

and seek the same boys who visit me in sleep,
leaving me wet with dreaming—

ravens croak like shifting gravel.
leaves sharp as arrowheads rustle.
this boy's mind grows furred,

feral near willows.

LATE AUGUST

far back. near the core.
among the earliest images.

a cobalt blue corduroy belt from a robe,
one end knotted to a bar on a crib,
the other leading to his mother
as she tries to nap on her bed.

when he cries, her hand
pulls the blue belt, causing the crib to sway back and forth.

it could've been late august—
a lack of certainty
shouldn't necessarily invalidate meaning.

the gold house.
the freshly tarred street.
the overgrown blackberry thicket.

it could've been late august—

isn't memory
finally more honest
than history?

for history's position,
that of
detachment, is never not a tactic, a posture.

memory falling
impressionistic, subjective.

it could've been late august—

the elaborate summer sun.
the rocking crib. a mother's—no,
my—my mother's patient hand

and the elaborate summer sun
dismantling itself outdoors.

FERRYMAN MARIA

sybille schmitz starred as maria
in the german reich's *ferryman maria.*

interiors filmed in berlin,
exteriors filmed in rural lower saxony.

a fable—a maiden outsmarts the figure of death.

my grandmother—also called maria—was assigned
as a cook in a labor camp.

my father remembers
going with her and the other kitchen workers and their young children
to take a shower.

after the war, my father would see similar showers in newsreels
descending, spewing zyklon b
for grandparent, parent, and child alike.

(what battles, sounds, brutalities continued for him
without abatement?)

why are these family stories necessary
to relay,
to confront again and again?

lines of difference—blur
then sharpen—between
labor camps, concentration camps, death camps.

does history offer—?

does memory abide—?

does cold philosophy even approach such—?

—a mourning dove walks along the edge of fence line,
flies into concrete.

it could be sky.

INTERCESSION

like a tragic heroine in early silent film,
grief claimed
my mother at birth.

life for her is puzzling when it is purely sweet,
so that she grows restless with it,
waiting for what she perceives to be

her true calling—
attention to sorrow.

it seems natural to my mother,
her looking after my uncle
who is dying as
she took care of their parents.

there is no surprise for her
that suffering

tries on, like
an article of clothing, another family member.

she understands suffering,
as a facet of love. it has

a rightful place at the family table.

ALLEGORY WITH
JAMES DEAN AS CAL AND
RICHARD DAVALOS AS ARON

dean sits on the edge of a turned-wood bed. his white shoes cast off to one side. shirtless, hunched over, he absentmindedly blows into a recorder. the mouthpiece parts his delicate lips. seven of his fingers and a thumb are arranged to correspond with the air holes along the red cedar shaft. davalos is stretched out in the room's second single bed. his arms disappear under a filmy cotton sheet. his bare nipples and muscular chest remain uncovered. davalos watches intently as dean fools with the woodwind instrument. a california breeze teases the half-drawn window shades.

KINDRED

this could be europe in '51. might be rome.
at a luxury apartment.

the doorbell rings. dinner guests begin to arrive.
the fireplace is lit.

during the meal's fish course, a twelve-year-old calls
for his mother. she excuses herself
from the long mahogany table.

on his bed, he cries. she chastises him.
such sensitivity, such unmanliness,
she scolds. threats of boarding school perhaps.
his face stares blankly.

the party continues. how much time passes?
wild-eyed, the maid rushes into the dining room.

the boy has fallen—sputtering like icarus,
over the building's ornate spiral stairwell rail,
plunging stories down to the marble lobby floor.

questions, strung together like a rosary, follow—
was this an accident or did the boy leap?
was such an act a release or a confession?
when did one last see such a flower caught in a steel trap?

a halo of five stars over slick winter roads.
thinning ice.

over a mouth, a hand, as the screaming stopped.

PRESSED

at nine, bought *my book*
of flowers by princess grace
in b. dalton. late
autumn 1980. sweet
men already infected.

INHERITANCE I

something is here with us, not kept at bay.
something moves just beyond, in corners.

fear as sickness.

intensity as revelation.

chase comfort in the near-human warmth
of towels removed from the dryer.

family is the accepted forum
for critique.

growing up with breaking glass.
uncles, aunts, cousins feeding on
past deeds. traumas. a shotgun in the mouth at fifty-nine.

another bakery birthday cake.
polaroid camera flashes
so bright,
blinding us to our places.

sage this house.
salt this stone land.

INHERITANCE 2

does that tolling
of church bells
indicate a funeral in progress?

•

whose name appears
on the original deed of this property?

•

can you hear
the pulsing?

can you hear
the blood?

•

where do you belong?

where are your people?

•

what chords
does the man in the skeleton mask
strum on his banjo?

•

are those party streamers
that the woman in black
unfurls from her hand?

•

who speaks
of the year's rye crop
poisoned by
dampness and bile?

•

must steep gables, casement windows
with diamond-shaped glass,
a central chimney, and charcoal clapboard
rend a family?

•

should the first period structure
be cleansed before winter solstice?

•

is the inventory the absent voice?

•

will cruelty wrenched
from its familial context
remain cruelty?

•

which daydream,
wrapped in mist,
is more real,
the past or the future?

•

how does a murky,
silvered photograph contain
truth or proof
of anything?

•

are you here at all?

or just a trick of
the camera as it takes in the light?

THE OUTER REACHES OF SOLITUDE;
OR, THE EXTREMES OF LONELINESS

grad school bloom. i rented in brooklyn heights.
you grew up nearby
on willow place
among harvard alums and greek revival town houses.

when we first met,
you just had come back from a year in paris
as an assistant to a staff writer for a glossy magazine.

we fell for each other hard. inseparable.
in and out
of record stores, used booksellers, vintage clothing shops.

i took to wearing bright clashing colors.
a bird of paradise.

summer became kicked aside flip-flops in central park.
you read aloud middle english. a longer-haired rupert brooke.
too beautiful for any battlefield.

for two weeks in march
we went to see every movie shown during a jean seberg retrospective;

over cherry pie at a diner down the street from film forum
you asked me,
"what is it that you need
more, me or poetry?"

in the dark apartment,
the torn foil squares of condom wrappers.

always you reached for
your boxer shorts
to wipe off the evidence, would wait
until home to wash away

obsessive love, white salt myths.

DOUBLE LIFE

this is something from a long time ago
before i ever knew you—

•

ellen anderson answers the door.
dropped off, anonymously, a snapshot
of her husband, brig, and another man in army dress uniforms
with hawaiian flower leis around their necks.
the word "forever" is written
under the men's smiling faces.

paper-clipped to the photograph,
a letter, in brig's handwriting:

"since coming home, i have realized that
what happened between us in hawaii
could not have happened but

for the war

and the exhaustion

and the loneliness.

i have a good normal life
here at home and i want to forget there was ever anything else."

•

brig's washington senate office. after hours.
his lightweight suit jacket hangs
on a louvered folding screen
by the restroom door.
a steel razor blade makes vertical slits
along the wrists of the junior senator from utah.
a black rotary telephone goes unanswered.

•

in club 602, groups of men huddle around a basement bar.
windowless. sinatra on the jukebox sings—

let me hear a voice,
a secret voice,

a voice that will say come to me.

NOCTURNE

of winter minutes—

walking home. the promenade at midnight.
others had gone.

left empty

by the taste of
his mouth.

LOVE FINDS ANTHONY PERKINS

the boathouse at midnight,
the silvered lake quiet.

i stare into the florida firmament,

trying to probe
its trembling depths, name its carnal forms,
while i wait for him.

we make sure to leave chase hall,
the freshman dormitory, at separate times.

moonlight builds
on the terra-cotta campus roofs.
spanish moss spews
from a stand of live oaks.

my college experience
winnows down to these meetings.

he appears
from waterlogged darkness
as if drawn to a wound.

a rural minister's son,
winter park, an uneasy metropolis to him.

for hours he imagines being
in his family's church, singing "a lamb goes
uncomplaining forth,"
singing "abide with us the day is waning."

what happens
when you discover a terrible utility
in hatred?

openly he pines for his girlfriend back home

as he fucks me in the boathouse.
the southern sky, scattered like
buckshot, savaged stars.

SEASONS

james ivory wrote the adapted screenplay
for *call me by your name.*

a movie categorized as a drama, a romance
between two men.

ivory's screenplay contained a narrator
that the film forgoes. is this
excision by director luca guadagnino
meant to honor
the mystery between two men?

is the inevitable love story
between the two main characters,
elio and oliver, mirrored
in the bounty surrounding them,
the italian summer landscape?

perhaps italy becomes a stand-in
for a narrator? or is italy in the 1980s,
itself, the seducer?

elio is seventeen and represents innocence.
oliver is twenty-five and represents experience.

a coming-of-age tale bound to a coming out tale.

when you and i met, we were the same age.
yet i was an elio; you were an oliver.

certain tropes, at least in our case,
such as innocence, such as experience,
resisted timekeeping.

today, from this other season,

with rows of daffodils illuminated for a moment
by headlights from a passing car, then swallowed
back into blackness,

i'm able to see your eventual absence
and its corresponding silence,

for what it was:
not cruelty, but gift.

you withdrew from my life; i was granted a space
to flourish in.
you gave me access
to my own heart,

in turn to wonder and sweetness—
love made available to me for the first time, completely.

melanie / tippi is stalked from above.
a predator's point of view. she drives her aston martin drophead coupe
past coastal ranches,
where lambs on foundling legs are rounded up for spring slaughter.
her full-length mink warms her. kitten heels,
leather purse, gold rope necklace compliment the green tweed suit she wears.

a fay green, like the paired
love birds that melanie / tippi transports in a gilded cage across bodega bay.
a short two-stroke journey. mitch / rod spots melanie / tippi
through binoculars, retreating in a motorboat, after leaving the birds
in the brenner farm house. a set built around
an already-existing abandoned cabin. love birds, caged—obvious symbolism.

later, children, including
little brenner sister, cathy / veronica, run from the 19th-century
potter school along a paved road while a camera trucks clumsily alongside.
the children run as if clouds of crows are sweeping down
and attacking them. boys in striped and checked shirts.
girls in solid skirts with bright cardigans.

mechanical crows are attached
to a few chosen child actors. live crows are tied, then untied,
from the playground jungle gym
and school roofline, some birds with stocking hoods masking their vision.
additional crows are added, as needed, via double printing
in post-production.

the separate location
towns of bodega and bodega bay meld, like a mirage,
at the studio into one true launching point of fear. the narrative crux,

a dime-store romance: ambivalent male meets self-possessed female. hitchcock's deadpan direction and spasm of images contort and convert nature's fury into a malady of eros, wounding us. to pleasure.

like proud parents in a 1970s family portrait, robert wagner and natalie wood,
    a movie star couple from the last gasp of hollywood's classic period
    on their second marriage to each other,
    stand off to one side, allowing
    the brand new arkla gas grill a place of prominence.
rj has his arm around natalie; her head tilts toward his broad chest.
    his chivalrous stance compliments her old-world features.
    smiles flash. such satisfaction
    rarely caught by a professional photographer on a product shoot.
yellow and azure cushions on white metal outdoor furniture.
    along a checkered tablecloth, a buffet. colorful salads. a pile of dinner rolls.
    a crock-pot—concealing baked beans?
    on the square grill, two cornish game hens, ears of corn.
in the advertisement, the tops of the resident palm trees go missing.
    beverly hills, like kindling, in the dried-up distance.
is this a set or really the wagner house on north canon drive,
    bought from patti page? where are their mercedes,
    the identical pair that include floor mats monogrammed
    with the celebrated twosome's interwoven initials?
clad in an earth-tone caftan, natalie is besieged
    by the surplus of exotic fabric. her neckline plummets
    in a sharp "v." a barefoot rj sports all jean.
    his sleeves rolled up. a red bandanna casually cinched around his neck.
stardom is the ultimate mythology of the self.
    perception buoys a movie star aloft on waves
    of time, floating the technicolor construction
    toward an accessible infinity
    as the actual body slips beneath chilled waters.
there, an in-ground pool, chlorine blue, not the november-black
    of seawater off the catalina coast.

waiting for the wagners, unseen,

natalie's favorite white wine, pouilly-fuissé, next to rj's bourbon-and-water.
their refilled glasses sweating on cork coasters.

NOTE TO SELF

sleigh bells, brief petals, bleat.
august strindberg snow.
my mind atomizes arctic terror.

is it ever spring?

•

stockholm in spring is lovely;
stockholm syndrome in spring is not.

•

a blue amaryllis, like water, in my lap
becomes
a hand mirror. narcissism's magic.

•

this swarm is marshaling—

to evade
itself.

JEAN SEBERG,
A MEMOIR
OF 1970

By 1970, movie star Jean Seberg's second marriage and film career were in free fall. In August, at age thirty-one, Seberg suffered the premature birth and death of a daughter. Publicly, she blamed the infant's early arrival on stress resulting from published reports that questioned her then unborn child's paternity. Privately, Seberg blamed herself for overdosing on sleeping pills only weeks before the premature birth. FBI files, made public, delineate the Bureau's covert smear campaign, under its Counterintelligence Program—COINTELPRO, against Seberg during this same period due to her direct support of the Black Panther Party. Throughout the late summer and fall of 1970, she suffered debilitating breakdowns. Most of November and much of December, Seberg spent shuttling between a clinic and her apartment in Paris.

Jean Seberg's unlikely rise to fame began in 1956, when, at seventeen, she was plucked out of Marshalltown, Iowa, by director Otto Preminger to star in his film *Saint Joan*. Soon after, with her nascent acting path at an impasse, she costarred in Jean-Luc Godard's unconventional first feature, *Breathless (À bout de souffle)*. Upon the film's release, Seberg found herself transformed into an internationally recognized symbol of the budding French New Wave.

JEAN SEBERG, A MEMOIR OF 1970
(VOLUME I)

CHAPTER I

during childhood ballet recitals i flickered fifth from the left.

my tutu, with a butterfly stitched on the bodice, now

droops from a sixpenny nail in an iowa attic.

flightless.

CHAPTER 2

i hold a buttercup under my chin to prove my unborn child will like
butter.

paternity rumors, atomic fallout,

irradiate the calendar.

CHAPTER 3

tabloid headline: iowa film queen expecting black panther baby!

adjacent headline: try serving bouillabaisse in a rustic tureen to wow
every guest at your next dinner party!

CHAPTER 4

on vacation in majorca, we sleep

separately. romain wants it this way.

our reunion,

a fabrication to safeguard a career, a name. presumably mine.

after midnight, an arabesque of moorish tiles lead me to his locked
bedroom door.

CHAPTER 5

vogue horoscope:

scorpio, *sign nothing nor seek favors—*

CHAPTER 6

before filming began on *lilith*, robert rossen had me visit a psychiatric
facility within range of washington, dc, to meet patients and
observe their behavior.

one occupant, a noted politician's sibling, claimed she was doing the
lord's work.

she knitted

colorful kidneys, small intestines, gallbladders,

ovaries, et cetera.

CHAPTER 7

i've become unmoored;

this can't be marseille, the fish stock tastes

like medicine.

CHAPTER 8

i heard rossen confess to the press why he hired me—*she's got that
flawed american-girl quality,*

sort of like a cheerleader who's cracked up.

CHAPTER 9

in 1957, i took the first husband, françois, home to meet my parents.

during that snowy trip, the whole family watched *the ed sullivan show*.
actress frances farmer made an appearance,

a comeback attempt, after being committed by her mother for years
   to a state mental institution.

frances: live on television, concave from fame.

CHAPTER 10

seven months pregnant.

the baby's removal imminent

and clinical, by easy latin allusion.

CHAPTER 11

at fourteen, i mailed an application to join the des moines, iowa,
   chapter of the naacp.

in my bedroom mirror,

i practiced acting exercises from my dog-eared copy of *othello*.

CHAPTER 12

in the cool dark of the orpheum movie theater—brando broods
   and anoints angst on the screen in *the men*, poitier pulses dignity
   and punctures racism in *no way out*.

how can marshalltown boys with sunburnt necks and letterman
    jackets compete?

CHAPTER 13

do you have to pet to be popular?

all the adults in marshalltown treat the label *a-girl-who-will*

as a legal term

or a medical diagnosis.

CHAPTER 14

thirteen blocks from the center of marshalltown

stands father's pride, seberg's pharmacy,

with its soda fountain, its post office, its peppermint candies, aspirin
    tablets, *photoplay* and *screenland* magazines.

i sip on an egg cream.

a middle child. in a middle-class life. in the middle of a state.
    in the middle of a country. in the middle of the american century.

CHAPTER 15

question: what was your iowa childhood like?

answer: an ode to creamed corn.

CHAPTER 16

airport remains popular showing across the country this august.

i'm back in a big hollywood production. all of marshalltown is proud
   of their third-rate jane fonda.

CHAPTER 17

on the news broadcast, the war metastasizes in vietnam.

twice an hour the wounded with stunted bandaged limbs

are carried from helicopters to temporary hospitals.

and in the states, also, daily battles continue

a black man is hounded like a criminal for cuddling in the park with
   a white woman. even love is dismembered there, here.

CHAPTER 18

j. edgar hoover's joke asks: what's black and white and dead all over?

the punch line: jean seberg's baby.

CHAPTER 19

you killed that motherfucking baby. you killed that little fucking piece of rubber

with them goddamn pills.

CHAPTER 20

along the rue du bac, the stale summer sun chokes in the deciduous
    trees—

CHAPTER 21

iowa curfews and sunday church services

closer each lutheran minute. a tornado touched down near winters dairy,

its erratic path toppling telephone poles and uprooting barn roofs,
    sparing certain cows and children, shattering used and unused
        milk bottles equally.

scourge and sepulcher. the eye of ahab's whale.

FOUND/ERED POEM

request (april 1970)

*bureau authority to forward a letter from a fictitious person to holly-
wood, california, gossip columnists to publicize the pregnancy of jean
seberg, well-known white movie actress, by* [REDACTED] *bpp*
[REDACTED] *to possibly cause her embarrassment and tarnish her
image with the general public. information from* [REDACTED] *indi-
cated that seberg was four months pregnant by* [REDACTED]

response (may 1970)

*to protect the sensitive source of information from possible compromise
and to insure the success of your plan,* [underlined] *bureau feels it would
be better to wait approximately two additional months* [underlining
ends] *until seberg's pregnancy would be obvious to everyone.*

[underlined] *note*

*jean seberg has been a financial supporter of the bpp and should be
neutralized. her current pregnancy by* [REDACTED] *while still married
affords an opportunity for such effort. the plan suggested by los angeles
appears to have merit except for the timing since the sensitive source
might be compromised if implemented prematurely.*

[stamped] *route in envelope*

JEAN SEBERG, A MEMOIR OF 1970 (VOLUME 2)

CHAPTER 1

it's a nearsighted sunday.

i wander around le marché aux puces de saint-ouen,

or as we call these markets, the fleas.

CHAPTER 2

i write in paris cafés.

this one has curtains like the plumage of the eastern goldfinch, my mother's favorite backyard bird.

i need to ask this—

be my stand-in. go to marshalltown's riverside cemetery. bring fresh violets for the baby girl.

talk to her so she is not lonesome.

CHAPTER 3

ignore all recent reports about the state of my darkened household.

like a verdigris door, soon the meadow will open. my proserpina will reappear.

milk has dried-up; i must buy infant formula instead.

a pewter owl sings a lullaby.

do not call. the telephone has grown ears.

CHAPTER 4

in a weekly advice column, one beauty industry expert
    recommends—

facelifts for the fall.

CHAPTER 5

trying to make order out of my life was like trying to pick up a jellyfish.

CHAPTER 6

this blue period picasso print "child with a dove."

after filming completed on *saint joan,* it was preminger's present of
    guilt for the incident on set.

joan at the stake.

armor gone. arms bound. i could not touch my own shorn scalp.

real flames, burning my hands and face

as the spider-god looked away.

CHAPTER 7

are these good days when baby nina never leaves my mind?

a clock marks the quarter hour; nurses scurry readying morning
medications.

all the patient rooms are decorated in soft yellows and creams, colors
selected to assure.

in the bath, my body withered and papery-white like the skeletal trees
edging the tuileries in winter.

—almost a fluttering inside me.

as if tiny nina still kept company.

CHAPTER 8

with the divorce final, romain and i divided our twelve-room rue du
bac apartment into separate dwellings.

this way diego, being eight, can go back and forth easily between us.

i moved out for a short time as renovations began.

and presto! i came back to a kitchen in my half of the world.

CHAPTER 9

night terrors. a grainy museum. bleared focus.

i'm led to a glass case.

residing within, the fossilized impression of a flower,

the travail of life—

strangely lasting, removed from human scale,

removed of time.

loss. loss. loss. deep, brine-black sea

close over me.

CHAPTER 10

i promise to donate all of nina's baby clothes as a sign of my
improving health.

the leaves of a large silver maple shimmer

like minnows moving through fresh water.

a warp in the mirror. a smudged thumbprint on a brass doorknob.
   the chill of flesh

minted into memory.

CHAPTER 11

yesterday, after reading mary shelley before bedtime, i dreamt that my
   little baby had merely been cold and that we rubbed her by the fire

and she lived.

CHAPTER 12

malcolm x montessori school shuttered its doors.

lack of financial support. a quick verdict: the community suffers.

hot meals and a chance to be heard—

why should compton kids find these

only in fairy tales and fifteen-cent comics?

CHAPTER 13

i'm heavy with guile, rat poison.

CHAPTER 14

at the fleas, under splintered sunlight. among tables

with bric-a-brac, a scarlet cardboard box full of images from the last
century.

i sift through example after example of what art scholars call spirit
photography.

in one carte de visite, a seated woman in an abundance of black silk
taffeta rigidly clasps a fan.

she betrays no single emotion.

over her left shoulder's opulent outline, a moon-faced toddler floats—

science and trickery unite what could no longer be united

in the guillotine-sweetened world.

A MARRIAGE TALE

CALIFORNIA

west—all the way.

our move still feels like yesterday,
although it has been ages
since we left the painted colonial house
and the massachusetts seaside town.

you, deep asleep in the bed next to me.
a compact dachshund snores
on the wool north star blanket at our feet.
a gentle whimper in her sleep—dreaming of what,
one of our evening walks
along the pacific at dillon beach?

we arrived to california in a drought year.
parched, like the local reservoirs, dairy cattle
dotted coastal hills eager for morning dew.
deer, with their fawns, fed
on the village's remaining ice plants.

marine layer obscures the long arm of point reyes.
the air weighty with eucalyptus,
to you a scent familiar
as the steamship-weathered pages
of your family album. familiar as the german community
you were born to in south america.

am i—are you—are we, together
falling into
our own biography?

propping open
the bedroom door, due to uneven beach house floors,
an antique bronze swan head. bought back east
at auction. its former life,
that of a water spigot for a grand garden.

nameless, flightless, yet yielding
to travel and homecoming
like driftwood.

this relic of some long-lost family, now anchor.

ANGLING

you're sleight of
hand—

my
saltwater eyes
parting

moon-
filled air
gasping

gills
am barbed

by you
cold

nirvana

THE CREATURE

from seas
of distance and darkness—

a shadow figure, a consciousness
creeps
toward physical flesh.

•

true vitruvian, shorthand for
proportionate, leanly muscled—

this male body
could be built
by joe dallesandro via paul morrissey via andy warhol.

after days of crypt death,
an inconsequential bump on left ankle
is lessened.

•

something in me was screaming
wake up—wake up—
but could not move, could not speak.

heart pound began.
faster and faster.

a dim mirage at the crossroads—a coach with pairs of horses
waiting, unclaimed.

•

am lazarus man. am four days

of trekking back—

through lunar barrenness
through dust, locusts, tears

then jacaranda trees sprouted,
as landscape transformed

itself into something
that shuddered with breath—

•

my victor. my maker. my frankenstein.

transfer consciousness to apparatus.
repair body.
transfer consciousness back to body.
conquer death.

an oyster slips back into its shell.

•

alive—

purple maytime. rock concert t-shirt weather. desire.
there is no further want of ritual shrouds.

morbidity and mortality weekly report.
reason, science—spark daybreak.

PHOSPHORUS AND HESPERUS,
MORNING STAR AND EVENING STAR

impaled forest—
boundary of disease, plague.

armies melt.
rival. lover.
walled kingdom.

bone break. bone break.
tender wake.

GEMINI

when you touch him.
when he touches you.

do you feel?
when your male hand
touches his male hand.

the stubble on
chin, jawline, face.
i have told,
lived this same story since—

on the double bed,
shed like snakeskin, his
corduroy blazer,
ted hughes black—

whiff of crow.
tin in the blood.

FILMED IN 35MM ON A MITCHELL

is this my life?
this feels like a movie set—

existing as a facsimile
of the actual world, an idealization
whose function
is deception.

opalescent sunlight
plaited purposely along a study's wainscoted walls.

atop a low, corner bookcase,
potted plants and miscellaneous knickknacks, including
a chipped medieval tile with heraldic beast,
its forepaws raised for attack or invite.

heywood-wakefield champagne finish
unifies the nonmatching desk and chair.

all objects like props deployed,
indebted to details in a shooting script.

static plot of flat blue,
resembling sky,
framed by closed windows.

such a smooth progression to time;
film winding through a camera.

then the flicker of movement, eucalyptus branches shifting—
from wind or special effects?
image and sound synchronized.

why do i prefer
illusion to fact? continual longing to closure,
to an ending?
the benefit that an ending affords—no further use for worry.

the tide retreats. godwits and plover actively
search wet sand for food.

maybe i'll go out. maybe i'll walk

with the two dogs on the widening beach. take in
the lion's shine and the day.

THE MIRROR

he pauses behind you. his shoulders sunburned
from his solo weekend
in palm springs.

your bodies fill the small
bureau mirror
as ceaseless appetite.

where were you
when, in the backroom of
a bar, he found
hallowedness—

fingers and their bitten discoveries,
mouths blooming together, the tumult
of male voices
heavy with breath
penetrating his mind, parsing
levels of desire?

are dante's
nine circles of hell
and nine spheres of heaven
distinct or
indistinguishable?

your separate forms
in the ring-shaped mirror
reflect a punishing truth—

what we are bred for, division.

GHOST

a thick fog. and the world so easily lost.

bone white mist envelops me,
a shroud.

erosion
of gull calls. anonymous,
lapping waves.

the red-walled shack blotted out
like prehistory.

a future lover, along with other party guests,
and my husband,
have followed me out to the dock.

one moment they're before me; then, they're dismantled
by the surrounding

holocaust
of white.

each dissolving into their own separate wilderness.

mechanical wail of a foghorn. ghost of a freighter.
how can they act this casual, still
chatting and laughing?

—don't you feel that sharp knife held to your throat?

NIGHT

you became real to me
the first time you were lost to me.

you were dressing
in front of the bedroom mirror,

studying your reflection
as if looking for signs
of what
passion had accomplished,

the idea of need extinguished—

damp skin of sheets; the rain lifting;
your bare shoulder blades,
their deceptive strength.

how could i not have been moved
to grief

to witness
your entry back into the unpardonable
structure of the present?

this was years ago.

should it matter to us
anymore? or that when my eyes were closed,
my left ear resting above your heart
heard: careful. careful.

FILM FESTIVAL

luminous mystery

a modern section of rome. vittoria strolls home
from her lover's apartment along the edge of a wide, empty street
passing under the dusky boughs of a conifer.
the streetlights are off. close by, a water tower rises.
contentment fills her. she sweeps her shawl
over the purple and burnt orange heads of roadside weeds and wild flowers.
a silence ripens in all things. reflected
in the late summer sprawl, finality and prospect.
night has faded. the dawn shimmers
like handblown glass, activated by light.

of drift and red bittersweet

italy, 1963—michelangelo antonioni directs his first film in color.

sky and marshland bleed gray like a late rothko painting.

the countryside around ravenna dominated by factories, refineries.

the horizon quartered by smokestacks. smoke clouds aimless. blackened shrubbery.

toward evening, a small hotel lobby.

a married woman (monica vitti) arrives through glass doors.

sofa, lounge chair, coffee table, curtains, even a rubber plant: all ashen.

on the third floor, outside his room, a male acquaintance (richard harris) waits for her.

his hands casually in his wool trouser pockets.

florescent lighting.

leaving the carpeted stairway, the woman staggers down the blanched corridor.

she enters his hotel room. he follows.

in front of almond walls, the woman takes off her corduroy coat.

on the desk, a square travel alarm clock.

she adjusts a few twigs in a translucent urn.

somewhere a tree rustles in wind, its sound a whispering, a catechism.

the woman allows the male acquaintance to remove her embroidered blouse.

his bed, arctic white.

antonioni shows the affair for what it is, cruel. and necessary.

dolorous mystery

papers in clipboards flutter in front of an open office window.
a phone lies off the hook.
vittoria's hair is disheveled. piero's narrow tie askew.
he walks her to the door. one more embrace.

the building's stairwell is dim and under repair.
she is alone again.

on her way down the stairs, she pauses, leaning against a wood plank,
to peer over her shoulder
back to the closed office door, back to
moments beyond reach.
the wood plank bites into her upper arm, trying
to leave a mark.

the death of
love,

the death of
what once felt boundless,
inexhaustible,
is accomplished.

the mind dissects
the heart, stills
its layered lives.

filmed through the lobby doorway—two lanes of moving traffic;
a woman holding a girl's hand as they wait to cross the street;
sunlight glinting from the metal grating of a store front.

vittoria turns and walks out of piero's building.
it is the last time. it is an ordinary afternoon.

A MARRIAGE TALE

intimate murmur of canal water—

reflected light
pooling on stone walls; pale blue
of a bed's headboard;
a tray with sweet bread, fresh fruit, two cups of espresso.

off-season and most guests are gone.
in the lobby, furniture
covered with white sheets, decorative rugs
rolled up and leaning into corners.
the hotel will be closing before long.

winter reclaims venice. clamminess
and dulling cold.

in a nearby church, beeswax candles
flicker, obscuring
patterns on the marble floor;
coins clatter,
dropping into a metal collection box.

infinite and finite geography,
this profusion of alleys and canals—

a couple wanders past
shop after empty shop
while another infidelity, as if audible,
trails after them in echoes
formed from their own laughter.

ALLEGORY WITHOUT
GWYNETH PALTROW AS PLATH AND
DANIEL CRAIG AS HUGHES

morning song. sunflowers. marginal winds.

four figures walk down a hill toward you, dear voyeur.

from left to right: young father, boy (toddler), girl (slightly older), young mother.

all hold hands. all make a chain. a handsome family.

sunflowers in foreground. mozart plays.

color field

wooded park. this is not jean renoir's *picnic on the grass.*

the young mother in a belted floral dress with a cardigan over her shoulders. she extinguishes the remains of a small campfire by pouring water on it.

both children under a makeshift canopy of mosquito netting held up by branches. the toddler squirms. his mother soothes him back to sleep. she rejoins her napping husband by the base of a leafy tree. the t-shirted husband wakes. they kiss.

pan of wooded park reveals a pond. other couples relaxing. an old man fishes.

the young family are leaving. the husband carries two large baskets. the wife carries the son. the girl ambles behind. each of them in their own world. the husband's work truck heads back to the city.

color field

post office, by an indoor telephone booth. the young husband meets a sunny, kittenish woman by chance.

strong attraction. close-up of a chagall stamp, "bride and groom of the eiffel tower."

midday. a street café. the young husband has a glass of wine while the endearing bit player from the post office drinks a cup of coffee.

in her modern apartment. blank walls and a vase of daisies. they begin an affair.

color field

the same wooded park. the young wife, again in a summer dress she has sewed herself, puts the children down for a nap under the canopy of mosquito netting. her young husband leans against the base of a tree with the daughter's doll in his hands, picking grass out of its long hair made of yarn.

the wife lies down on a blanket next to her husband. for comfort she removes a sheer scarf from her head that she had twisted into a head-band. an intense discussion in hushed voices follows. at one point the wife takes the doll out of her husband's hands. tall, dry grasses in afternoon light. he confesses to his affair with the other woman. he confesses his happiness. mozart plays. the young wife undresses as her young husband kisses her face, her neck, her arms with exuberance. she continues to undress. he tosses aside the light jacket he is sitting on, it lands on the grasses. after sex, the young husband sleeps. the young wife stares at you, dear voyeur. her breasts casually exposed. her head rests on her young husband's shoulder and on his dark chest hair.

bird song. the daughter wakes and calls for her mother. the young father is still asleep under a blanket. his young wife is no longer beside him. the daughter runs over to him as he awakes. she whines for her mother.

the young father and the two children search the wooded park. he calls his wife's name repeatedly. he inquires as he passes others in the wooded park. suddenly he leaves the children with a woman reading a glossy magazine. he bolts toward a crowd at the pond's edge. the group of strangers move aside. the young wife's dead body has been pulled from the pond. her soaked, leaden dress. no shoes. *wintering.*

MOON AND PALM TREE

in the three a.m. hour

he shifts
in his sleep—

and his arm
rests

against me

how did it become
in the long shadows

of the bedroom—

your arm, your
body

that moved toward
me

again?

TOMALES BAY

I .

your body is the

        one true door to the golden

west; all roads lead to

              dunes, pine, fog, sea, salty sun—

              all roads lead to

paradise.

2 .

is it true—tell me,

lie to me—

to abandon   the past
is to

forgive

oneself?

3.

our bodies hammer,
                    hammer
and unlock

                              the dawn—

we are made sun kings.

a black trans am drives toward a rental cabin in the powdery california mountains. mist rises over the rolling terrain. four male friends, graduating from trade school, carry their suitcases up a path. one slips a bit on icy pavement. they track snow onto the orange wall-to-wall shag carpeting as they proceed into the cabin. two take off down ski jackets and start a fire in the fireplace. the other two pivot around and go for a snowball fight. the short, redheaded guy feeds a nut to a squirrel on the porch. eventually, they all settle down for a meal of scrambled eggs and beer. a massive tv rests in the center of the sparsely furnished rec room. after eating, the young men pop in a video tape. on the tv, a handsome blond in his early twenties finishes zipping up a red and navy blue wetsuit. he and another sun-bleached friend paddle out on surfboards and ride cold water waves. later, they arrive at a bungalow. a muscle man in plaid with facial hair shows them into his house. they are there to stain the stripped oak floors. they will be paid twenty-five dollars each. the man in faded plaid catches them waxing their surfboards instead of working. somehow the trio ends up on a bed, sans clothing. mark scott solo, the straight star of this pre-condom classic, bottoms on all fours, the mustached man bent over him. swim trunks have left a distinct tan line. solo's face is flushed; he flinches as the beefy brunet enters him roughly.

THE DEATH OF CLASSICAL CINEMA

immutable gospel:
with birth, we are made mortal.

profound distress follows—

how to cope with
such monolithic truth?

we search for associations.
make metaphors.

—is it easier this way?

consider gable and monroe
in *the misfits*.
their final scene,
their last picture.

they move slowly
through craggy desert
in the cab of a battered pickup,
smiling, allowing

some tethered star
to guide them home.

ANNIVERSARY

over the hundred-year-old neighborhood, san diego
dusk descends
this october hour—

we watch the garden lights turn on
here and there,
shining like
the small unripe globes on the orange tree's boughs.

an opened wine bottle rests on a talavera tiled step,
beside us.

married life is a curious journey—

as with those ancestors that came before,
we move deeper into adulthood with bodies yoked to aging;
traveling an ambiguous
path, an invisible scar.

both benefits and losses accrue
in piles, recollections
of spent yet colorful leaves.

inside your whisper's subtle wit,
accepted differences.
and dusty springfield, recorded decades ago, wafts through our window,
a throaty, undiminished song.

NOTES

GHOST IN THE GRAVEYARD: Modifies, in the first line, a phrase from a Swedish travel poster.

ALLEGORY WITH JAMES DEAN AS CAL AND RICHARD DAVALOS AS ARON: Scene cut from Elia Kazan's *East of Eden*.

KINDRED: Roberto Rossellini's *Europa '51* (*Europe '51*).

DOUBLE LIFE: Otto Preminger's film *Advise & Consent*. Quotes language from the film, including the Frank Sinatra song "Heart of Mine" (Music: Jerry Fielding; Lyrics: Ned Washington).

HITCHCOCK: Alfred Hitchcock's *The Birds*.

JEAN SEBERG, A MEMOIR OF 1970 (VOLUME I): Cites horoscope from a 1970 issue of *Vogue*. Quotes director Robert Rossen. Uses the 1950s phrases *do you have to pet to be popular* and *a-girl-who-will* from *Facts of Life and Love for Teen-Agers* by Evelyn Millis Duvall. Quotes Hakim Jamal's purported remarks to Seberg about the death of her daughter.

FOUND/ERED POEM: Source COINTELPRO document, dated May 6, 1970, between FBI director J. Edgar Hoover and the Los Angeles Division.

JEAN SEBERG, A MEMOIR OF 1970 (VOLUME 2): Employs quote from *Self-Portrait* by Gene Tierney with Mickey Herskowitz. Alters a Mary Shelley quote published in *The Journals of Mary Shelley: 1814–1844* edited by Paula R. Feldman and Diana Scott-Kilvert.

[REEL TWO]
A MARRIAGE TALE

PHOSPHORUS AND HESPERUS, MORNING STAR AND EVENING STAR: Personified in the 1881 Pre-Raphaelite painting by Evelyn De Morgan.

GHOST: Michelangelo Antonioni's *Deserto Rosso (Red Desert)*.

FILM FESTIVAL: *Luminous Mystery*: Antonioni's *L'Eclisse (The Eclipse)*. *Of Drift and Red Bittersweet*: *Deserto Rosso (Red Desert)*. *Dolorous Mystery*: *L'Eclisse (The Eclipse)*.

A MARRIAGE TALE: Nicolas Roeg's *Don't Look Now*.

ALLEGORY WITHOUT GWYNETH PALTROW AS PLATH AND DANIEL CRAIG AS HUGHES: Agnès Varda's *Le Bonheur (Happiness)*. Begins and ends with the words Sylvia Plath selected as first and last poem titles in her original manuscript, *Ariel and Other Poems*.

ALLEGORY WITH SNOW AND SURF: William Higgins's *Malibu Days/ Big Bear Nights*.

ACKNOWLEDGMENTS

I wish to thank:

Tracy—for vital kinship, a bulwark against the tides, poetic and otherwise;

Alice, Emily, Jenn—each for a critical eye on these poems and for steadfast friendship;

Linda Gregg—more than a mentor, rather, a luminous guide;

finally, my mother and father.

My appreciation to the Fine Arts Work Center for its fellowship.

Acknowledgement is made to the following publications in which these poems first appeared (some in earlier versions):

"Night" in *The New Yorker*;

"Film Festival: Luminous Mystery" (under "Film Study: Transcendence") in *Guernica*;

"Film Festival: Of Drift and Red Bittersweet" (under "The Affair") in *Agni*;

"Film Festival: Dolorous Mystery" (under "Italian Movie") in *The Yale Review*;

"Allegory Without Gwyneth Paltrow as Plath and Daniel Craig as Hughes" in *Plath Profiles*;

"Love Finds Anthony Perkins"; "Angling"; and with "Phosphorus and Hesperus, Morning Star and Evening Star" and "Gemini" (under one title "Gemini") in *ArLiJo* (*The Arlington Literary Journal*);

"Jean Seberg, A Memoir of 1970" (under "The Cantos of Jean Seberg") in *Clockhouse*.

JEB

ABOUT THE AUTHOR

DAVID SEMANKI holds an MFA from Columbia University. While an editor, he conceived of, wrote the commentary for, and shepherded into publication Sylvia Plath's *Ariel: The Restored Edition*. Semanki's poetry has appeared in a variety of publications, including *The New Yorker*, *The Yale Review*, *The American Poetry Review*, *The New York Times Book Review*, and *The Paris Review*. He is the literary executor for the estate of poets Linda Gregg and Jack Gilbert. After years living in California, he has returned to rural New England.

Made in the USA
Middletown, DE
21 March 2024